United States
Department of
Agriculture

Forest Service

**Southern
Research Station**

Resource Bulletin
SRS–95

Virginia's Timber Industry—
An Assessment of Timber Product
Output and Use, 2001

Michael Howell and
Charles W. Becker

The Authors:

Michael Howell is a Resource Analyst with the Forest
Inventory and Analysis Research Work Unit, Southern
Research Station, U.S. Department of Agriculture, Forest
Service, Knoxville, TN 37919. **Charles W. Becker III** is a
Staff Forester - Utilization and Marketing with the Virginia
Department of Forestry, Charlottesville, VA 22903.

August 2004

Southern Research Station
P.O. Box 2680
Asheville, NC 28802

Foreword

This report contains the findings of a 2001 canvass of all primary wood-using plants in Virginia, and presents changes in product output and residue use since 1999. It complements the Forest Inventory and Analysis periodic inventory of volume and removals from the State's timberland. The canvass was conducted to determine the amount and source of wood receipts and annual timber product drain, by county, in 2001 and to determine interstate and cross-regional movement of industrial roundwood. Only primary wood-using mills were canvassed. Primary mills are those that process round-wood in log or bolt form or as chipped roundwood. Examples of industrial roundwood products are saw logs, pulpwood, veneer logs, poles, and logs used for composite board products. Mills producing products from residues generated at primary and secondary processors were not canvassed. Trees chipped in the woods were included in the estimate of timber drain only if they were delivered to a primary domestic manufacturer.

A 100-percent canvass of all wood processors in Virginia was conducted in 2002 to obtain information for 2001. In addition, roundwood from out-of-State mills known to be using logs or bolts harvested from Virginia timberland was incorporated into Virginia production estimates. Each mill was canvassed by mail or through personal contact at plant locations. Telephone contacts followed mailed questionnaire responses when additional information or clarification of a response was necessary. In the event of a nonresponse, data collected in previous surveys were updated using current data collected for mills of similar size, product type, and location. Surveys for all timber products other than pulpwood began in 1965, and are currently conducted every 2 years.

Pulpwood production data were taken from an annual canvass of all southern pulpmills. Medium density fiberboard, insulating board, and hardboard plants were included in this survey.

Acknowledgments

The authors thank John A. Scrivani for review and comments; Dumitru Salajanu for the maps; Anne Jenkins, Charlene Walker, and Lyn Thornhill for tables, graphs, and statistical checking; and Paul Smith, Diana Corbin, and Louise Wilde for editorial review, styling, and publication of this report.

The Southern Research Station gratefully acknowledges the cooperation and assistance provided by the Virginia Department of Forestry in collecting mill data. Appreciation is also extended to forest industry and mill managers for providing timber products information.

Contents

[a] All tables in this report are available in Microsoft® Excel workbook files. Upon request, these files will be supplied on 3½-inch diskettes.

 The use of trade or firm names in this publication is for reader information and does not imply endorsement by the U.S. Department of Agriculture of any product or service.

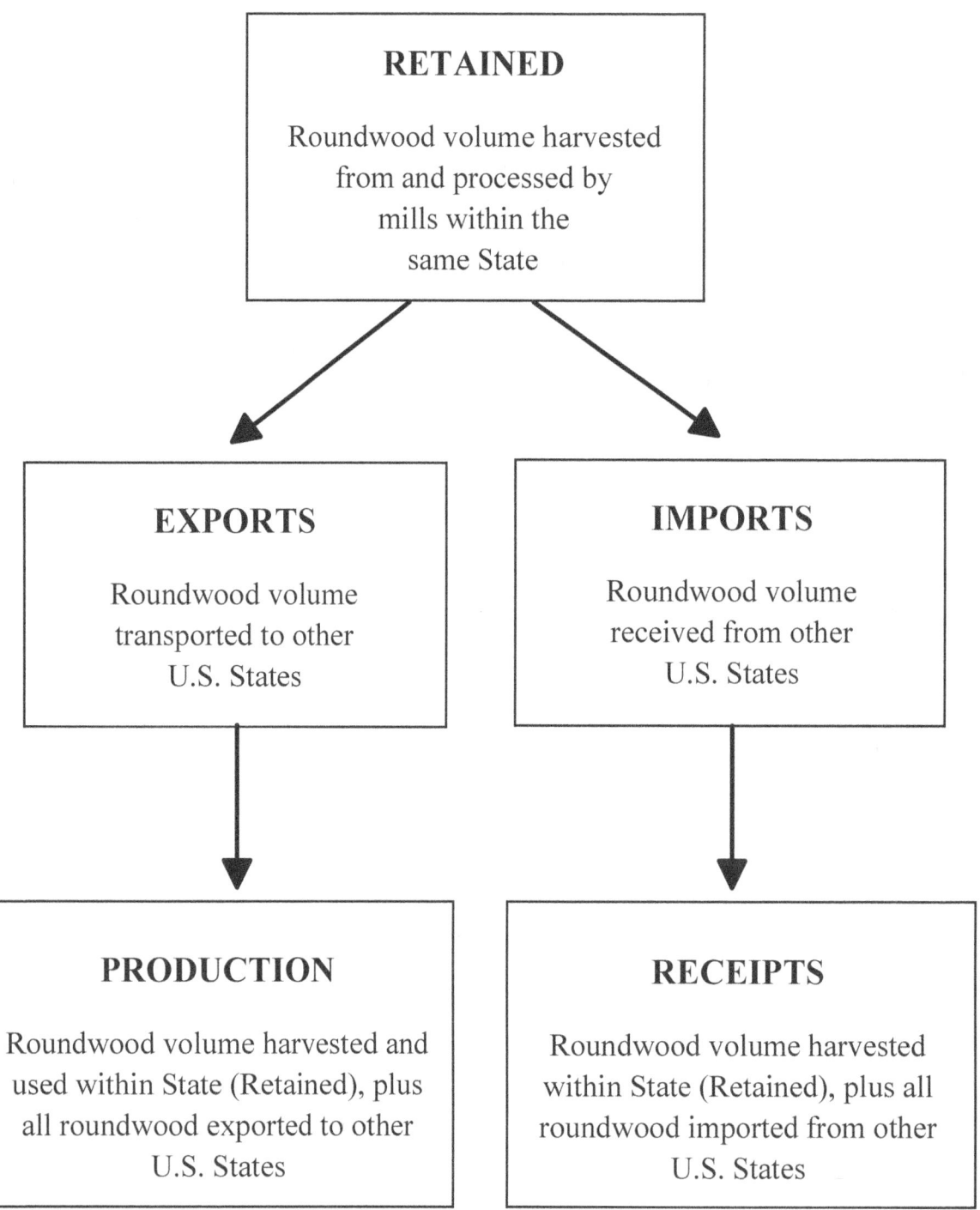

Figure 1—Movement of roundwood exports and imports within the United States.

Virginia's Timber Industry— An Assessment of Timber Product Output and Use, 2001

Michael Howell and Charles W. Becker

Output of Industrial Timber Products

Note: Certain terms used in this report—retained, export, import, production, and receipts—have specialized meanings and relationships unique to the Forest Inventory and Analysis Units across the country that deal with timber products output (fig. 1).

All Products

- Between 1999 and 2001, the combined industrial timber products output (TPO) from roundwood and plant byproducts increased 2 percent, from 658 to 673 million cubic feet.

- TPO from roundwood remained stable at 492 million cubic feet while output of plant byproducts increased 9 percent, from 167 to 181 million cubic feet.

- Output of softwood roundwood products declined 3 percent to 254 million cubic feet, while output of hardwood roundwood products increased 3 percent to 238 million cubic feet (fig. 2).

- Figures 3 and 4 display softwood and hardwood county-level intensity of roundwood production for all industrial products across Virginia. The data are depicted in cubic feet produced per acre of census land area. Counties with the highest production intensity are depicted in the darker shades. For softwoods the darkest shade represents more than 30 cubic feet of production per acre, while for hardwoods the darkest shade represents more than 18 cubic feet per acre.

- Saw logs and pulpwood were the principal roundwood products in 2001. Combined output of these two

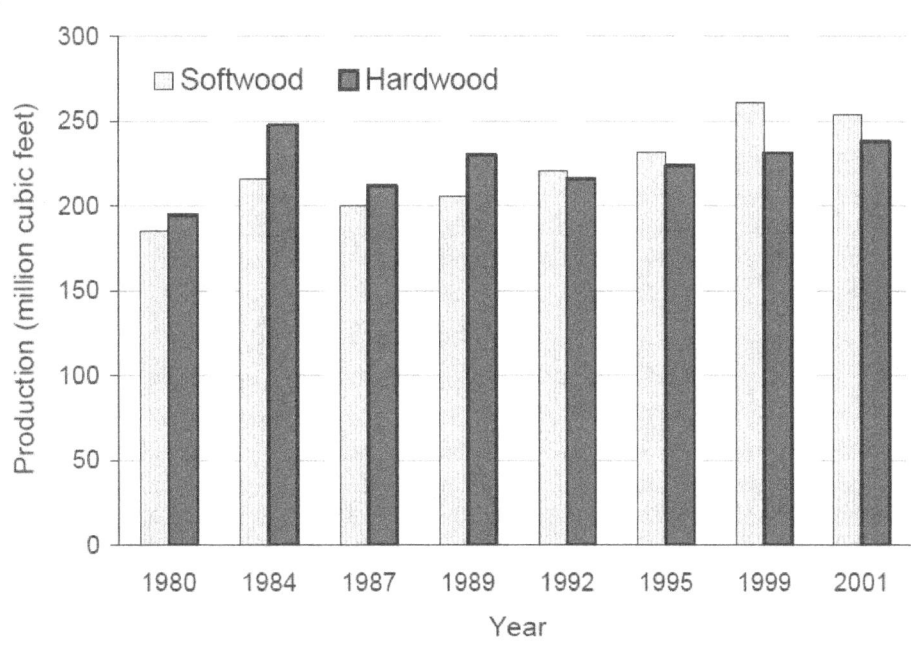

Figure 2—Roundwood production for all products by species group and year (see page 10 for references for individual years).

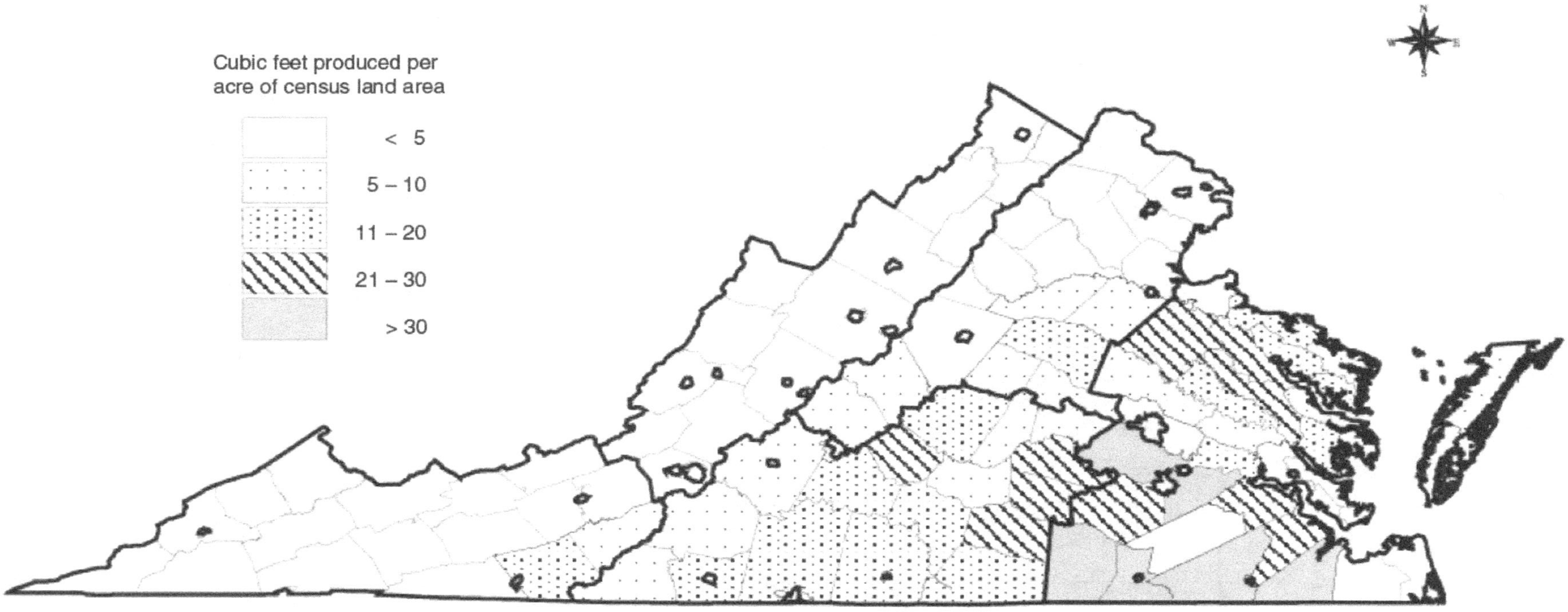
Cubic feet produced per
acre of census land area
< 5
5 – 10
11 – 20
21 – 30
> 30
N
W
E
S

Figure 3—Intensity of roundwood softwood output for all industrial products in Virginia by county, 2001.

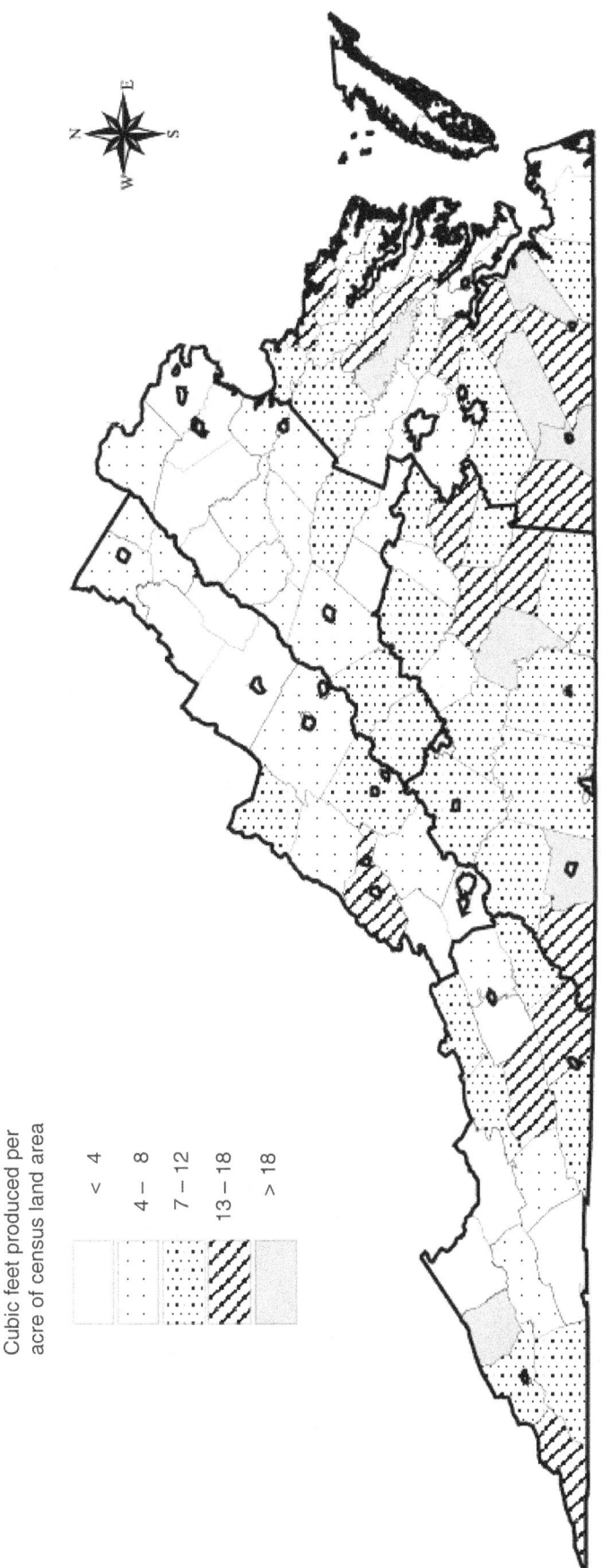

Cubic feet produced per
acre of census land area

< 4

4 – 8

7 – 12

13 – 18

> 18

Figure 4—Intensity of roundwood hardwood output for all industrial products in Virginia by county, 2001.

products totaled 423 million cubic feet and accounted for 86 percent of the State's total roundwood output (fig. 5).

- Total receipts at Virginia mills, which included roundwood harvested and retained in the State and roundwood imported from other States, increased 1 percent to 492 million cubic feet. At the same time, the number of primary roundwood-using plants in Virginia declined from 290 in 1999 to 248 in 2001.

Saw Logs

- Saw logs accounted for 51 percent of the State's total roundwood products. Output of softwood saw logs increased 404 thousand cubic feet to 116 million cubic feet (633 million board feet, International ¼-inch rule), while that of hardwood saw logs increased 5 percent to 137 million cubic feet (834 million board feet, International ¼-inch rule) (fig. 6).

- In 2001, Virginia had 217 sawmills, a net loss of 37 mills since 1999. The total number of sawmills does not include several one-man sawmills not picked up in this survey. Total saw-log receipts increased 9 million cubic feet to 253 million cubic feet. Softwood saw-log receipts

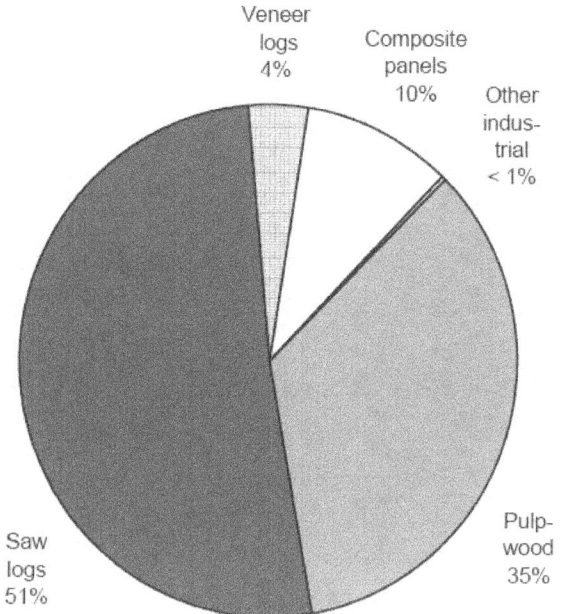

Total 492 million cubic feet

Figure 5—Roundwood production by type of product, 2001.

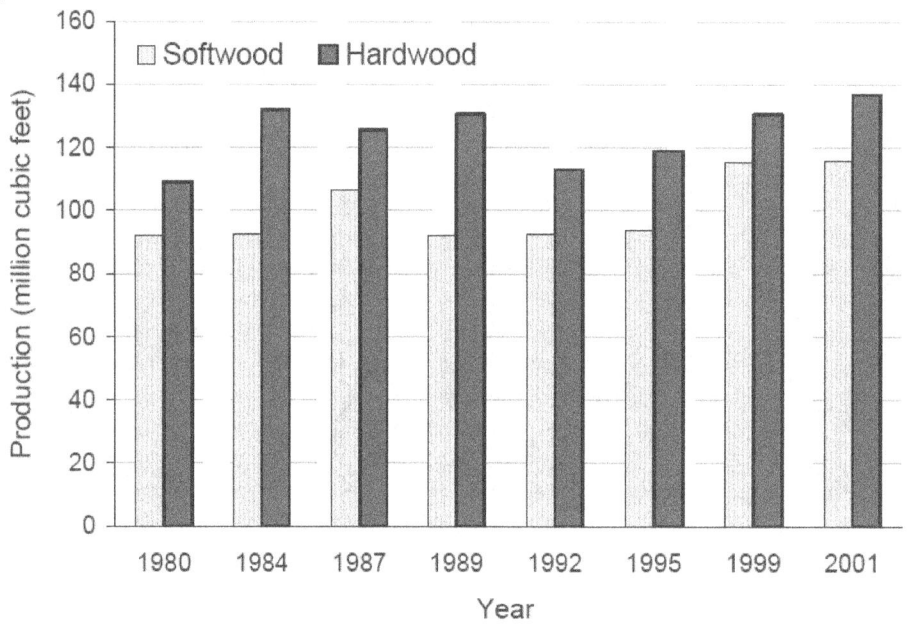

Figure 6—Roundwood saw-log production by species group and year (see page 10 for references for individual years).

4

decreased 1 percent to 115 million cubic feet, while hardwoods increased 8 percent to 138 million cubic feet. Of the 217 mills operating in 2001, 19 percent had receipts of less than 1 million board feet, while 43 percent, or 93 mills, had receipts greater than 5 million board feet.

- Virginia retained 89 percent of its saw-log production for domestic manufacture, with saw-log imports exceeding exports by 640 thousand cubic feet in 2001.

Pulpwood

- Pulpwood production, including chipped roundwood, decreased 5 million cubic feet to 170 million cubic feet and accounted for 35 percent of the State's total roundwood TPO. Softwood output decreased 9 percent to 89 million cubic feet (1.2 million cords), while hardwood output increased 5 percent to 81 million cubic feet (1.1 million cords) (fig. 7).

- Nine pulpmill facilities were operating and receiving roundwood in Virginia in 2001, the same as in 1999. Total pulpwood receipts for these mills increased 7

million cubic feet to 181 million cubic feet, accounting for 37 percent of total receipts for all mills.

- Eighty-four percent of roundwood cut for pulpwood was retained for processing at Virginia pulpmills. Roundwood pulpwood accounted for 36 percent of total known exports and 50 percent of total imports. Roundwood pulpwood exports amounted to 27 million cubic feet, while imports amounted to 38 million cubic feet, making the State a net importer of roundwood pulpwood.

Veneer Logs

- Output of veneer logs in 2001 totaled 19 million cubic feet and accounted for 4 percent of the State's total roundwood TPO volume. Softwood veneer-log production decreased 6 percent to 13 million cubic feet (81 million board feet, International ¼-inch rule), while output of hardwood veneer-log production decreased 2 percent to 6 million cubic feet (36 million board feet, International ¼-inch rule) (fig. 8).

- The number of veneer mills operating in Virginia was down from seven to five since 1999. Total receipts for veneer logs decreased 7 percent to18 million cubic feet.

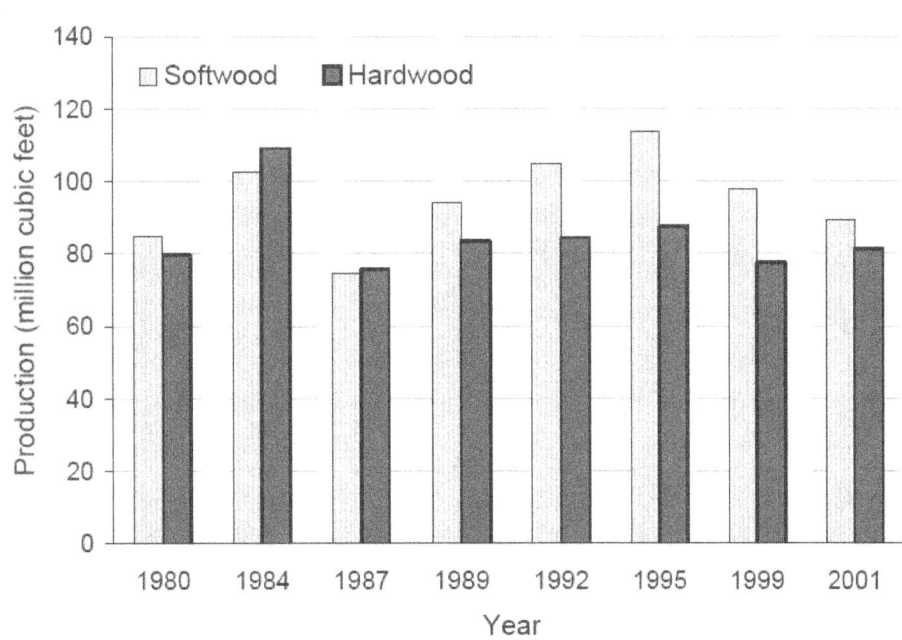

Figure 7—Roundwood pulpwood production by species group and year (see page 10 for references for individual years).

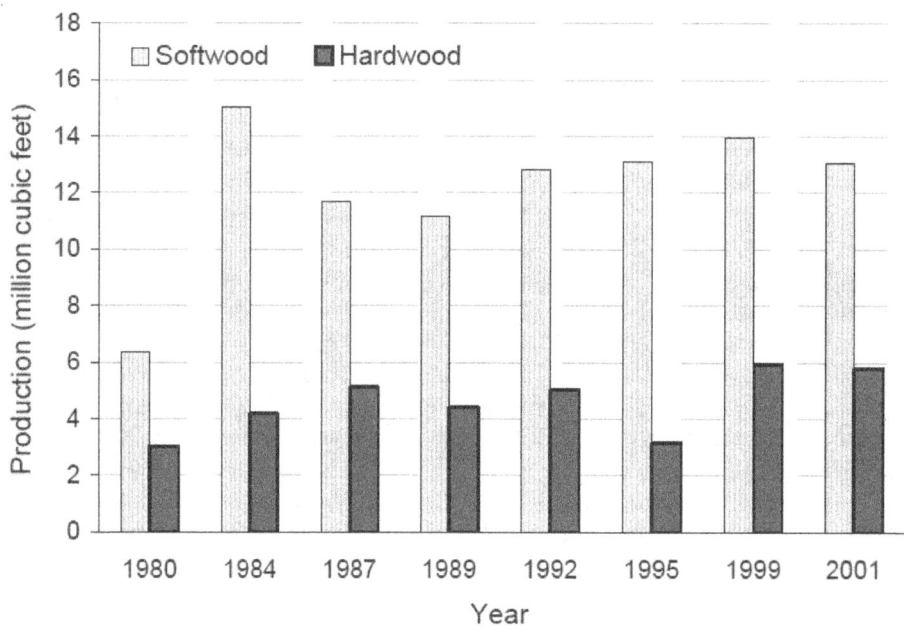

Figure 8—Roundwood veneer-log production by species group and year (see page 10 for references for individual years).

- Virginia retained 70 percent of its veneer-log production for processing at domestic veneer mills. Imports amounted to 5 million cubic feet, while exports totaled 6 million cubic feet.

Composite Panels

- Roundwood harvested from Virginia's forests for composite panels increased 5 percent and totaled 48 million cubic feet. Softwood output was up 10 percent to 34 million cubic feet (464 thousand cords), while hardwood production decreased 5 percent to 14 million cubic feet (181 thousand cords) (fig. 9).

- The number of composite panel mills operating in Virginia decreased from four to three. Total receipts for these mills were 38 million cubic feet, or about 8 percent of the State's total receipts.

- Seventy-one percent of the roundwood production harvested for composite panels was retained for processing at Virginia's mills. Imports amounted to 4 million cubic feet, while exports totaled 14 million cubic feet, making the State a net exporter of logs used for composite panels.

Other Industrial Products

- Roundwood harvested for other industrial uses such as poles, posts, mulch, firewood, logs for log homes, and all other industrial products totaled 2 million cubic feet and accounted for about one-half of 1 percent of the State's total TPO. Softwood made up 81 percent of the other industrial product volume.

- The number of plants producing other industrial products decreased from 16 to 14. Combined receipts of other industrial products from softwood and hardwood totaled 3 million cubic feet.

- Virginia was a net importer of roundwood used for other industrial products; of the 319 thousand cubic feet imported, 95 percent was softwood.

Plant Byproducts

- In 2001, processing of primary products in Virginia mills generated about 185 million cubic feet of wood and bark residues. Coarse residues from all primary products amounted to 75 million cubic feet, while bark volume

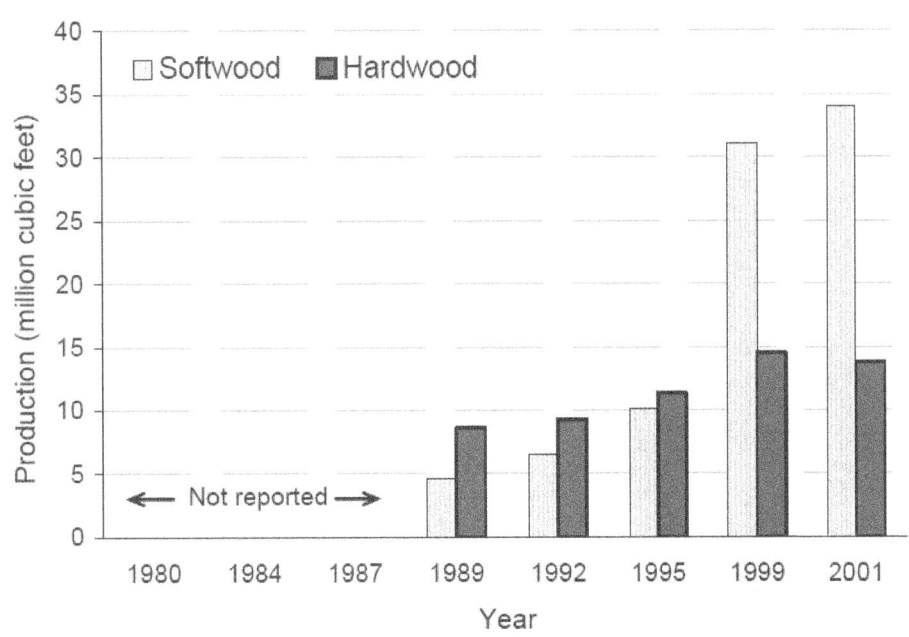

Figure 9—Roundwood production for composite panels by species group and year (see page 10 for references for individual years).

totaled 52 million cubic feet. Collectively, sawdust and shavings made up 32 percent of total residues, or 58 million cubic feet (fig. 10).

- Virtually all the wood and bark residues were used for a product: about 2 percent were not used, while 40 percent of the residues were used for industrial fuel (fig. 11). Sixty-four million cubic feet, or 86 percent, of the coarse residues were used for fiber products. Most of the bark was used for industrial fuel or other miscellaneous products, while 67 percent of the sawdust and shavings were used for industrial fuel.

- The processing of saw logs generated 146 million cubic feet of mill residues, accounting for 79 percent of the total residues produced (fig. 12).

Regional Trends

Output of industrial roundwood products decreased in the Northern Piedmont and Southern Piedmont regions and increased in all other regions with the Southern Mountain region having the largest increase at 12 percent.

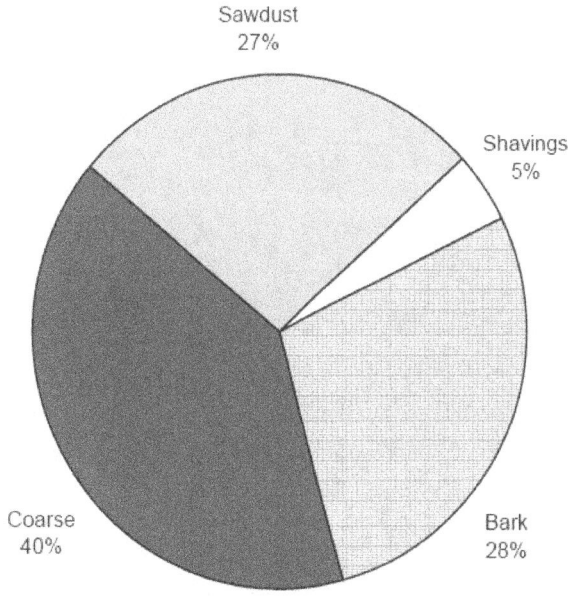

Total 185 million cubic feet

Figure 10—Primary mill residue by residue type, 2001.

7

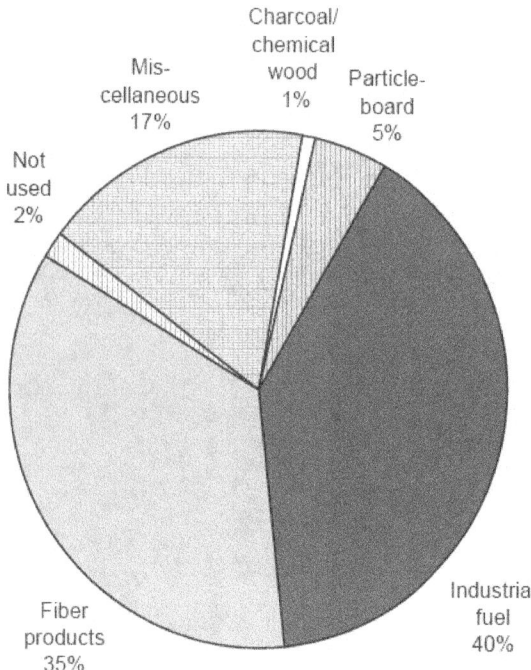

Total 185 million cubic feet

Figure 11—Disposal of residue by product, 2001.

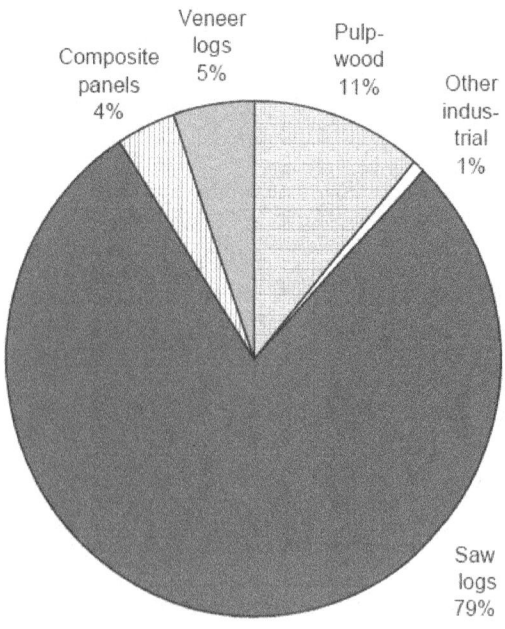

Total 185 million cubic feet

Figure 12—Primary mill residue produced by roundwood type, 2001.

Coastal Plain Region

- Roundwood output from the Coastal Plain region totaled 207 million cubic feet, up 6 percent since 1999.

- Pulpwood accounted for 39 percent of the region's TPO and 47 percent of the State's roundwood pulpwood output. The 96 million cubic feet of saw logs accounted for 46 percent of the total roundwood output for the region.

- In the Coastal Plain region, 53 primary wood-using plants were operating during 2001, 8 less than in 1999: 41 sawmills, 5 pulpmills, 2 veneer or plywood mills, 1 composite panel mill, and 4 other miscellaneous mills. These mills processed 42 percent of the State's total roundwood output.

Southern Piedmont Region

- Roundwood output from the Southern Piedmont region totaled 150 million cubic feet, a decrease of 8 percent.

- Saw-log production of 71 million cubic feet accounted for 48 percent of the region's total roundwood output. Production of pulpwood dropped to 51 million cubic feet and accounted for 34 percent of the region's total roundwood output.

- The 85 mills operating in the Southern Piedmont region in 2001 included 78 sawmills, 2 veneer or plywood mills, 2 pulpmills, 2 composite panel mills, and 1 other miscellaneous mill.

Northern Piedmont Region

- Roundwood output from the Northern Piedmont region totaled more than 45 million cubic feet, down 10 percent. Roundwood production from this region accounted for 9 percent of the total roundwood TPO for the State.

- Pulpwood production declined by 10 percent to 19 million cubic feet, accounting for 42 percent of the region's total TPO. Saw-log production of 23 million cubic feet accounted for another 51 percent of the region's total roundwood output.

- The 40 primary wood-using plants operating in the Northern Piedmont region included 33 sawmills, 1 pulpmill, and 6 other miscellaneous mills.

Northern Mountain Region

- Roundwood output from the Northern Mountain region totaled 30 million cubic feet, an increase of 7 percent.

- Saw-log production remained stable at 16 million cubic feet, accounting for 55 percent of the region's total roundwood output. Production of pulpwood increased 9 percent to 12 million cubic feet and accounted for 40 percent of the region's total roundwood output.

- In the Northern Mountain region, 30 primary wood-using plants were operating during 2001: 25 sawmills, 1 veneer mill, 1 pulpmill, and 3 other miscellaneous mills.

Southern Mountain Region

- Roundwood output from the Southern Mountain region totaled 60 million cubic feet, an increase of 12 percent.

- Saw-log production increased 18 percent to 46 million cubic feet and accounted for 76 percent of the region's total roundwood output. Pulpwood production was up 42 percent and accounted for 14 percent of the region's total TPO. Composite panel production decreased 61 percent to 2 million cubic feet.

- In the Southern Mountain region, 40 sawmills were operating during 2001.

Total Roundwood Output

Using the most recent inventory data for Virginia, product output by source, ownership, and detailed species group was estimated.

Source

- In addition to the 492 million cubic feet of roundwood output for industrial roundwood, an estimated 51 million cubic feet was harvested for domestic fuelwood, bringing Virginia's total roundwood output to 543 million cubic feet.

- An estimated 93 percent of total roundwood output was considered growing-stock volume (sawtimber and poletimber) from timberland sources. Other sources

(such as saplings; stumps, tops, and limbs of trees on timberland; and trees on nonforest land) contributed an estimated 40 million cubic feet, or 7 percent of total roundwood output (fig. 13).

Ownership

- An estimated 456 million cubic feet, or 84 percent, of the total roundwood output came from nonindustrial private forest lands. Forest industry lands contributed 68 million cubic feet, or 12 percent of the output. Public lands made up the remaining 4 percent, or 20 million cubic feet (fig. 14).

Species

- The loblolly and shortleaf pine group provided the most volume of any softwood species group, accounting for 70 percent of the total softwood output. The other yellow pine types accounted for 24 percent of the softwood output (fig. 15). In hardwoods, the red oak and white oak groups combined accounted for 134 million cubic feet, or 47 percent of total hardwood output (fig. 16). Yellow-poplar accounted for another 55 million cubic feet, or 19 percent of total hardwood output.

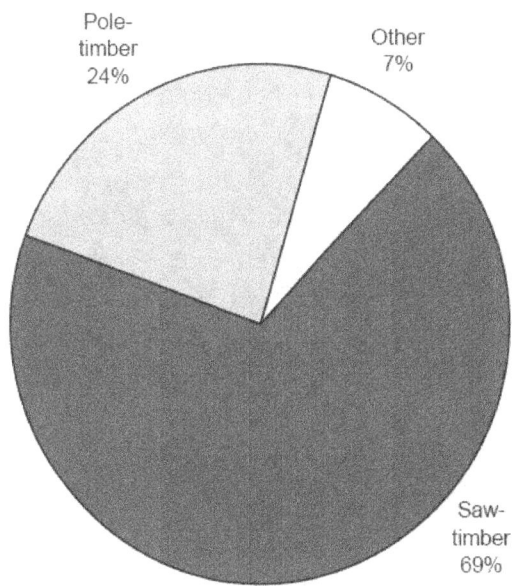

Total 543 million cubic feet

Figure 13—Roundwood output by source, 2001.

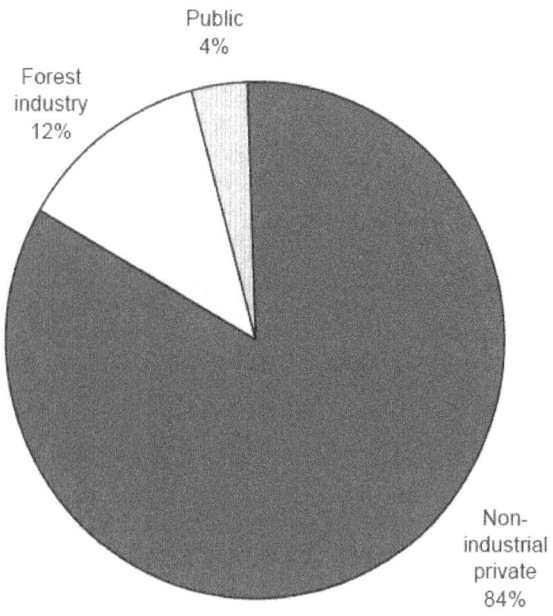

Total 543 million cubic feet

Figure 14—Roundwood output by ownership, 2001.

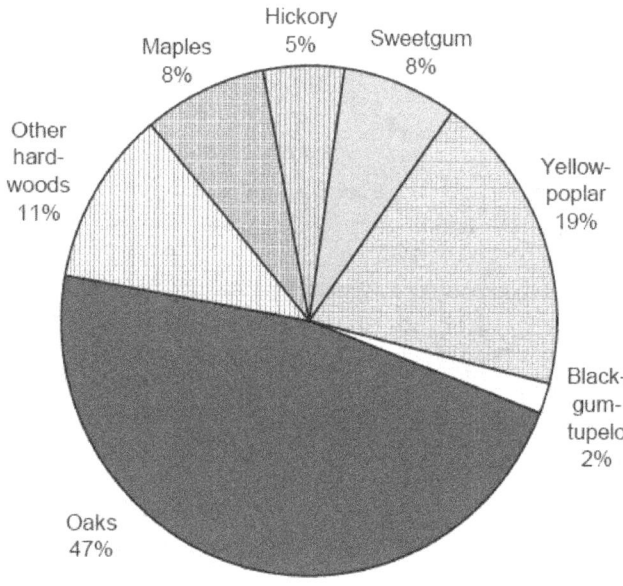

Total 284 million cubic feet

Figure 16—Roundwood output by hardwood species group, 2001.

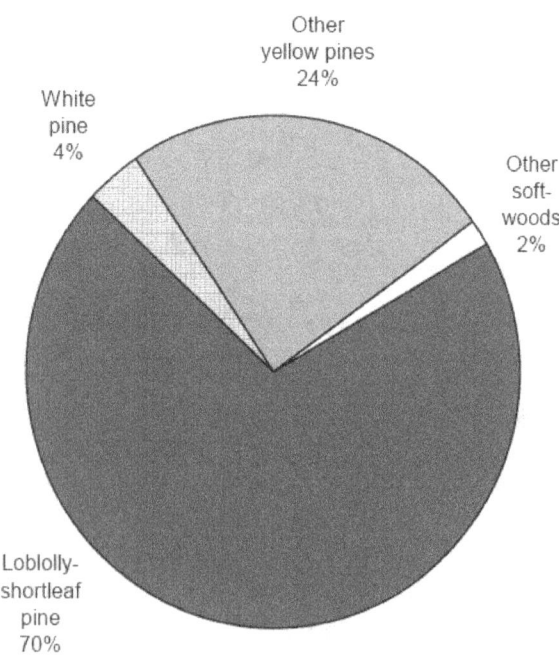

Total 259 million cubic feet

Figure 15—Roundwood output by softwood species group, 2001.

References

Hutchins, Cecil C., Jr. 1992. Changes in output of industrial timber products in Virginia, 1987–1989. Resour. Bull. SE–129. Asheville, NC: U.S. Department of Agriculture, Forest Service, Southeastern Forest Experiment Station. 18 p. [1987, 1989].

Johnson, Tony G. 1994. Virginia's timber industry—an assessment of timber product output and use, 1992. Resour. Bull. SE–145. Asheville, NC: U.S. Department of Agriculture, Forest Service, Southeastern Forest Experiment Station. 32 p. [1992].

Johnson, Tony G.; Jenkins, Anne; Scrivani, John A.; Foreman, J. Michael. 1997. Virginia's timber industry—an assessment of timber product output and use, 1995. Resour. Bull. SRS–19. Asheville, NC: U.S. Department of Agriculture, Forest Service, Southern Research Station. 37 p. [1995].

U.S. Department of Agriculture, Forest Service. Product drain by county, product, and species. 6 p. Unpublished data. On file with: Southern Research Station, Forest Inventory and Analysis Research Work Unit, 4700 Old Kingston Pike, Knoxville, TN 37919. [1980, 1984].

Welch, Richard L.; Bellamy, Thomas R. 1980. Changes in output of industrial timber products in Virginia, 1976–1978. Resour. Bull. SE–54. Asheville, NC: U.S. Department of Agriculture, Forest Service, Southeastern Forest Experiment Station. 21 p. [1978].

Definition of Terms

Board foot. A unit of measure applied to lumber that is 1-foot long, 1-foot wide, and 1-inch thick (or its equivalent) and also associated with roundwood as to its potential yield of such products.

Byproducts. Primary wood products, e.g., pulp chips, animal bedding, and fuelwood, recycled from mill residues.

Composite panels. Roundwood products manufactured into chips, wafers, strands, flakes, shavings, or sawdust and then reconstituted into a variety of panel and engineered lumber products.

Consumption. The quantity of a commodity, such as pulpwood, utilized by a particular mill or group of mills.

Drain. The volume of roundwood removed from any geographic area where timber is grown.

Exports. The volume of domestic roundwood utilized by mills outside the State where timber was cut.

Fiber products. Byproducts used in the manufacture of pulp, paper, paperboard, and composite products, such as chipboard.

Fuelwood production. The volume of roundwood harvested to produce some form of energy, e.g., heat, steam, in residential, industrial, or institutional settings.

Growing-stock removals. The growing-stock volume removed from poletimber and sawtimber trees in the timberland inventory. (Note: Includes volume removed for roundwood products, logging residues, and other removals.)

Growing-stock trees. Living trees of commercial species classified as sawtimber, poletimber, saplings, and seedlings. Growing-stock trees must contain at least one 12-foot or two 8-foot logs in the saw-log portion, currently or potentially (if too small to qualify). The log(s) must meet dimension and merchantability standards and have, currently or potentially, one-third of the gross board-foot volume in sound wood.

Growing-stock volume. The cubic-foot volume of sound wood in growing-stock trees at least 5.0 inches d.b.h. from a 1-foot stump to a minimum 4.0-inch top d.o.b. of the central stem.

Hardwoods. Dicotyledonous trees, usually broadleaf and deciduous.

Soft hardwoods. Hardwood species with an average specific gravity of 0.50 or less, such as gums, yellow-poplar, cottonwoods, red maple, basswoods, and willows.

Hard hardwoods. Hardwood species with an average specific gravity greater than 0.50, such as oaks, hard maples, hickories, and beech.

Imports. The volume of domestic roundwood delivered to a mill or group of mills in a specific State but harvested outside that State.

Industrial fuelwood. A roundwood product, with or without bark, used to generate energy at a manufacturing facility such as a wood-using mill.

Industrial roundwood products. Any primary use of the main stem of a tree, such as saw logs, pulpwood, veneer logs, intended to be processed into primary wood products such as lumber, wood pulp, sheathing, at primary wood-using mills.

International ¼-inch rule. A log rule or formula for estimating the board-foot volume of logs, allowing ½-inch of taper for each 4-foot length. The rule appears in a number of forms that allow for kerf. In the form used by FIA, a ¼-inch of kerf is assumed. This rule is used as the USDA Forest Service standard log rule in the Eastern United States.

Log. A primary forest product harvested in long, primarily 8-, 12-, and 16-foot lengths.

Logging residues. The unused merchantable portion of growing-stock trees cut or destroyed during logging operations.

Merchantable portion. That portion of live trees 5.0 inches d.b.h. and larger between a 1-foot stump and a minimum 4.0-inch top d.o.b. on the central stem. That portion of primary forks from the point of occurrence to a minimum 4.0-inch top d.o.b. is included.

Merchantable volume. Solid-wood volume in the merchantable portion of live trees.

Noncommercial species. Tree species of typically small size, poor form, or inferior quality that normally do not develop into trees suitable for industrial wood products.

Nonforest land. Land that has never supported forests and land formerly forested where timber production is precluded by development for other uses.

Nongrowing-stock sources. The net volume removed from the nongrowing-stock portions of poletimber and sawtimber trees (stumps, tops, limbs, cull sections of central stem) and from any portion of a rough, rotten, sapling, dead, or nonforest tree.

Other forest land. Forest land other than timberland and productive reserved forest land. It includes available and reserved forest land that is incapable of producing annually 20 cubic feet per acre of industrial wood under natural conditions because of adverse site conditions such as sterile soils, dry climate, poor drainage, high elevation, steepness, or rockiness.

Other products. A miscellaneous category of roundwood products, e.g., cooperage, excelsior, shingles, and mill residue byproducts (charcoal, bedding, mulch, etc.).

Other removals. The growing-stock volume of trees removed from the inventory by cultural operations such as timber stand improvement, land clearing, and other changes in land use, resulting in the removal of the trees from timberland.

Other sources. (See: Nongrowing-stock sources.)

Ownership. The property owned by one ownership unit, including all parcels of land in the United States.

National forest land. Federal land that has been legally designated as national forests or purchase units, and other land under the administration of the Forest Service, including experimental areas and Bankhead-Jones Title III land.

Forest industry land. Land owned by companies or individuals operating primary wood-using plants.

Nonindustrial private forest (NIPF) land. Privately owned land excluding forest industry land.

Corporate. Owned by corporations, including incorporated farm ownerships.

Individual. All lands owned by individuals, including farm operators.

Other public. An ownership class that includes all public lands except national forests.

Miscellaneous Federal land. Federal land other than national forests.

State, county, and municipal land. Land owned by States, counties, and local public agencies or municipalities, or land leased to these governmental units for 50 years or more.

Plant residues. Wood material generated in the production of timber products at primary manufacturing plants.

Coarse residues. Material, such as slabs, edgings, trim, veneer cores and ends, which is suitable for chipping.

Fine residues. Material, such as sawdust, shavings, and veneer residue, which is not suitable for chipping.

Plant byproducts. Residues (coarse or fine) used in the further manufacture of industrial products for consumer use or as fuel.

Unused plant residues. Residues (coarse or fine) that are not used for any product, including fuel.

Poletimber-size trees. Softwoods 5.0 to 8.9 inches d.b.h. and hardwoods 5.0 to 10.9 inches d.b.h.

Posts, poles, and pilings. Roundwood products milled (cut or peeled) into standard sizes (lengths and circumferences) to be put in the ground to provide vertical and lateral support in buildings, foundations, utility lines, and fences. May also include nonindustrial (unmilled) products.

Primary wood-using plants. Industries that convert round-wood products (saw logs, veneer logs, pulpwood, etc.) into primary wood products, such as lumber, veneer or sheathing, wood pulp.

Production. The total volume of known roundwood harvested from land within a State, regardless of where it is consumed. Production is the sum of timber harvested and used within a State, and all roundwood exported to other States.

Pulpwood. A roundwood product that will be reduced to individual wood fibers by chemical or mechanical means. The fibers are used to make a broad generic group of pulp products that includes paper products, as well as fiberboard, insulating board, and paperboard.

Receipts. The quantity or volume of industrial roundwood received at a mill or by a group of mills in a State, regardless of the geographic source. Volume of roundwood receipts is equal to the volume of roundwood retained in a State plus roundwood imported from other States.

Retained. Roundwood volume harvested from and processed by mills within the same State.

Rotten trees. Live trees of commercial species not containing at least one 12-foot saw log, or two noncontiguous saw logs, each 8 feet or longer, now or prospectively, primarily because of rot or missing sections, and with less than one-third of the gross board-foot tree volume in sound material.

Rough trees. Live trees of commercial species not containing at least one 12-foot saw log, or two noncontiguous saw logs, each 8 feet or longer, now or prospectively, primarily because of roughness, poor form, splits, and cracks, and with less than one-third of the gross broad-foot tree volume in sound material; and live trees of noncommercial species.

Roundwood (roundwood logs). Logs, bolts, or other round sections cut from trees for industrial manufacture or consumer uses.

Roundwood chipped. Any timber cut primarily for industrial manufacture, delivered to nonpulpmills, chipped, and then sold to pulpmills for use as fiber. Includes tops, jump sections, whole trees, and pulpwood sticks.

Roundwood products. Any primary product, such as lumber, veneer, composite panels, poles, pilings, pulp, or fuelwood that is produced from roundwood.

Roundwood product drain. That portion of total drain used for a product.

Salvable dead trees. Standing or downed dead trees that were formerly growing stock and considered merchantable. Trees must be at least 5.0 inches d.b.h. to qualify.

Saplings. Live trees 1.0 to 5.0 inches d.b.h.

Saw log. A roundwood product, usually 8 feet in length or longer, processed into a variety of sawn products such as lumber, cants, pallets, railroad ties, and timbers.

Saw-log portion. The part of the bole of sawtimber trees between a 1-foot stump and the saw-log top.

Saw-log top. The point on the bole of sawtimber trees above which a conventional saw log cannot be produced. The minimum saw-log top is 7.0 inches d.o.b. for softwoods and 9.0 inches d.o.b. for hardwoods for FIA standards.

Sawtimber-size trees. Softwoods 9.0 inches d.b.h. and larger and hardwoods 11.0 inches d.b.h. and larger.

Sawtimber volume. Growing-stock volume in the saw-log portion of sawtimber-sized trees in board feet (International ¼-inch rule).

Seedlings. Trees less than 1.0 inch d.b.h. and greater than 1 foot tall for hardwoods, greater than 6 inches tall for softwood, and greater than 0.5 inch in diameter at ground level for longleaf pine.

Select red oaks. A group of several red oak species composed of cherrybark, Shumard, and northern red oaks. Other red oak species are included in the "other red oaks" group.

Select white oaks. A group of several white oak species composed of white, swamp chestnut, swamp white, chinkapin, Durand, and bur oaks. Other white oak species are included in the "other white oaks" group.

Softwoods. Coniferous trees, usually evergreen, having leaves that are needles or scalelike.

Standard cord. A unit of measure applied to roundwood, usually bolts or split wood. It is a stack of wood 4 feet high, 4 feet wide, and 8 feet long encompassing 128 cubic feet of wood, bark, and air space. This usually translates to approximately 75.0 to 81.0 cubic feet of solid wood for pulpwood, because pulpwood is more uniform.

Standard unit. A unit measure applied to roundwood timber products. Board feet (International ¼-inch rule) is the standard unit used for saw logs and veneer; cords are used for pulpwood, composite panel, and fuelwood; hundred pieces for poles; thousand pieces for posts; and thousand cubic feet for all other miscellaneous forest products.

Timberland. Forest land capable of producing 20 cubic feet of industrial wood per acre per year and not withdrawn from timber utilization.

Timber products. Roundwood products and byproducts.

Timber products output. The total volume of roundwood products from all sources plus the volume of byproducts recovered from mill residues (equals roundwood product drain).

Timber removals. The total volume of trees removed from the timberland inventory by harvesting, cultural operations such as stand improvement, land clearing, or changes in land use. (Note: Includes roundwood products, logging residues, and other removals.)

Tree. Woody plants having one erect perennial stem or trunk at least 3 inches d.b.h., a more or less definitely formed crown of foliage, and a height of at least 13 feet (at maturity).

Upper-stem portion. The part of the main stem of sawtimber trees above the saw-log top and the minimum top diameter of 4.0 inches outside bark, or to the point where the main stem breaks into limbs.

Utilization studies. Studies conducted on active logging operations to develop factors for merchantable portions of trees left in the woods (logging residues), logging damage, and utilization of the unmerchantable portion of growing-stock trees and nongrowing-stock trees.

Veneer log. A roundwood product either rotary cut, sliced, stamped, or sawn into a variety of veneer products such as plywood, finished panels, veneer sheets, or sheathing.

Weight. A unit of measure for mill residues, expressed as oven-dry tons (2,000 oven-dry pounds).

Conversion Factors[a]

Saw logs	
Softwood	0.18282 cubic foot = 1 board foot
	5.47 board feet = 1 cubic foot
Hardwood	0.16393 cubic foot = 1 board foot
	6.10 board feet = 1 cubic foot
Veneer logs	
Softwood	0.16129 cubic foot = 1 board foot
	6.20 board feet = 1 cubic foot
Hardwood	0.16000 cubic foot = 1 board foot
	6.25 board feet = 1 cubic foot
Pulpwood[b]	
Softwood	73.3 cubic feet per cord
Hardwood	76.1 cubic feet per cord

[a] Conversion factors vary with stem size (d.b.h.) and species. The factors shown are for trees of average diameters removed in Virginia during the most recent survey period.

[b] Cubic feet of solid wood per cord.

Index of Tables

Table 1—Output of industrial products by product and species group, Virginia, 1999 and 2001

Product and species group	Year		Change	Percent change
	1999	2001		
	thousand cubic feet			
Saw logs				
Softwood	115,299	115,703	404	0.4
Hardwood	130,578	136,729	6,151	4.7
Total	245,877	252,432	6,555	2.7
Veneer logs				
Softwood	13,947	13,075	-872	-6.3
Hardwood	5,947	5,810	-137	-2.3
Total	19,894	18,885	-1,009	-5.1
Pulpwood[a]				
Softwood	97,664	89,200	-8,464	-8.7
Hardwood	77,536	81,246	3,710	4.8
Total	175,200	170,446	-4,754	-2.7
Composite panels				
Softwood	31,106	34,066	2,960	9.5
Hardwood	14,552	13,779	-773	-5.3
Total	45,658	47,845	2,187	4.8
Other industrial				
Softwood	2,411	1,878	-533	-22.1
Hardwood	2,521	429	-2,092	-83.0
Total	4,932	2,307	-2,625	-53.2
All industrial				
Softwood	260,427	253,922	-6,505	-2.5
Hardwood	231,134	237,993	6,859	3.0
Total	491,561	491,915	354	0.1
Byproduct output				
Softwood	83,392	86,534	3,142	3.8
Hardwood	83,132	94,939	11,807	14.2
Total	166,524	181,473	14,949	9.0
Total output				
Softwood	343,819	340,456	-3,363	-1.0
Hardwood	314,266	332,932	18,666	5.9
Total	658,085	673,388	15,303	2.3

[a] Includes roundwood delivered to nonpulpmills, then chipped and sold to pulpmills (3,693,000 cubic feet in 1999 and 2,734,000 cubic feet in 2001).

Table 2—Roundwood receipts by product and species group, Virginia, 1999 and 2001

Product and species group	Year			
	1999	2001	Change	Percent change
	thousand cubic feet			
Saw logs				
Softwood	115,492	114,580	-912	-0.8
Hardwood	128,833	138,492	9,659	7.5
Total	244,325	253,072	8,747	3.6
Veneer logs				
Softwood	17,294	16,519	-775	-4.5
Hardwood	2,054	1,399	-655	-31.9
Total	19,348	17,918	-1,430	-7.4
Pulpwood[a]				
Softwood	86,628	80,043	-6,585	-7.6
Hardwood	87,311	101,147	13,836	15.8
Total	173,939	181,190	7,251	4.2
Composite panels				
Softwood	32,569	29,670	-2,899	-8.9
Hardwood	14,078	8,029	-6,049	-43.0
Total	46,647	37,699	-8,948	-19.2
Other industrial				
Softwood	2,940	2,077	-863	-29.4
Hardwood	2,521	444	-2,077	-82.4
Total	5,461	2,521	-2,940	-53.8
Total output				
Softwood	254,923	242,889	-12,034	-4.7
Hardwood	234,797	249,511	14,714	6.3
Total	489,720	492,400	2,680	0.5

[a] Includes roundwood delivered to nonpulpmills, then chipped and sold to pulpmills (4,629,000 cubic feet in 1999 and 4,283,000 cubic feet in 2001).

Table 3—Number of primary wood-using plants by industry, Virginia, 1978–2001

Industry	Year							
	1978	1980	1984	1987	1989	1995	1999	2001
Sawmills	324	392	419	355	323	254	254	217
Veneer or plywood mills	12	12	12	10	10	8	7	5
Pulpmills	8	9	9	9	9	9	9	9
Composite panel mills	0	0	0	1	3	3	4	3
Other mills	18	24	22	19	24	15	16	14
All plants	362	437	462	394	369	289	290	248

Table 4—Roundwood receipts by sawmill size, Virginia, 1999 and 2001

Sawmill size class[a]	1999			2001		
	Number of mills	Thousand board feet	Percent of volume	Number of mills	Thousand board feet	Percent of volume
million board feet						
< 1.0	67	22,697	2	42	14,242	1
1.0 – 4.99	94	265,231	19	82	229,599	15
5.0 – 9.99	55	369,991	26	52	347,605	24
> 10	38	758,791	53	41	879,177	60
Total	254	1,416,710	100	217	1,470,623	100

[a] Based on volume received as opposed to actual capacity.

18

Table 5—Roundwood receipts by species and type of mill, Virginia, 2001

Species	All mills	Sawmills	Veneer mills Pine plywood	Veneer mills Other veneer	OSB[a] and panels	Pulpwood[b]	Other mills
			thousand cubic feet				
Softwood							
Yellow pine	152,179	103,916	16,225	291	29,670	NA	2,077
White pine	9,398	9,395	0	3	0	NA	0
Cedar	57	57	0	0	0	NA	0
Cypress	408	408	0	0	0	NA	0
Other softwood	804	804	0	0	0	NA	0
Unclassified	80,043	0	0	0	0	80,043	0
Total softwoods	242,889	114,580	16,225	294	29,670	80,043	2,077
Hardwood							
Blackgum and tupelo	550	430	0	3	117	NA	0
Soft maple	3,380	3,260	0	3	117	NA	0
Sweetgum	3,074	2,918	0	0	156	NA	0
Yellow-poplar	42,408	41,955	0	62	391	NA	0
Other soft hardwood	14,984	7,736	0	0	7,248	NA	0
Hickory	3,418	3,330	0	14	0	NA	74
Red oak	39,906	39,581	0	266	0	NA	59
White oak	26,045	25,703	0	304	0	NA	38
Other hard hardwood	14,599	13,579	0	747	0	NA	273
Unclassified	101,147	0	0	0	0	101,147	0
Total hardwoods	249,511	138,492	0	1,399	8,029	101,147	444
All species	492,400	253,072	16,225	1,693	37,699	181,190	2,521

NA = not applicable.

[a] OSB = oriented strand board.

[b] Collected only by softwood and hardwood and includes roundwood chipped.

Table 6—Industrial roundwood movement by year and species group, Virginia, 1999 and 2001

Year	Production	Exported to other States	Retained	Imported from other States	Receipts
		thousand cubic feet			
		Softwood			
1999	260,427	34,992	225,435	29,488	254,923
2001	253,922	43,422	210,500	32,389	242,889
		Hardwood			
1999	231,134	29,210	201,924	32,873	234,797
2001	237,993	31,261	206,732	42,779	249,511
		All species			
1999	491,561	64,202	427,359	62,361	489,720
2001	491,915	74,683	417,232	75,168	492,400

Table 7—Industrial roundwood movement by product and species group, Virginia, 2001

Product and species group	Production	Exported to other States	Retained	Imported from other States	Receipts
			thousand cubic feet		
Saw logs					
Softwood	115,703	18,832	96,871	17,709	114,580
Hardwood	136,729	9,035	127,694	10,798	138,492
Total	252,432	27,867	224,565	28,507	253,072
Veneer logs					
Softwood	13,075	84	12,991	3,528	16,519
Hardwood	5,810	5,642	168	1,231	1,399
Total	18,885	5,726	13,159	4,759	17,918
Pulpwood[a]					
Softwood	89,200	16,442	72,758	7,285	80,043
Hardwood	81,246	10,676	70,570	30,577	101,147
Total	170,446	27,118	143,328	37,862	181,190
Composite panels					
Softwood	34,066	7,959	26,107	3,563	29,670
Hardwood	13,779	5,908	7,871	158	8,029
Total	47,845	13,867	33,978	3,721	37,699
Other industrial					
Softwood	1,878	105	1,773	304	2,077
Hardwood	429	0	429	15	444
Total	2,307	105	2,202	319	2,521
All products					
Softwood	253,922	43,422	210,500	32,389	242,889
Hardwood	237,993	31,261	206,732	42,779	249,511
Total	491,915	74,683	417,232	75,168	492,400

[a] Includes roundwood chipped.

Table 8—Saw-log volume by destination, source, and species group, Virginia, 2001

Destination and source	All species	Species group	
		Softwood	Hardwood
	thousand cubic feet		
Virginia (retained)	224,565	96,871	127,694
Exports to:			
Kentucky	252	0	252
North Carolina	23,364	18,782	4,582
Tennessee	2,713	13	2,700
West Virginia	1,538	37	1,501
Total	27,867	18,832	9,035
Imports from:			
Kentucky	1,914	440	1,474
Maryland	619	13	606
North Carolina	21,732	16,679	5,053
Pennsylvania	40	16	24
Tennessee	1,464	222	1,242
West Virginia	2,738	339	2,399
Total	28,507	17,709	10,798

Table 9—Veneer volume by destination, source, and species group, Virginia, 2001

Destination and source	All species	Species group	
		Softwood	Hardwood
	thousand cubic feet		
Virginia (retained)	13,159	12,991	168
Exports to:			
Georgia	1,862	84	1,778
Kentucky	219	0	219
North Carolina	3,600	0	3,600
West Virginia	45	0	45
Total	5,726	84	5,642
Imports from:			
Foreign	2	0	2
Illinois	40	0	40
Indiana	103	2	101
Kentucky	149	0	149
Maine	7	0	7
Maryland	8	0	8
Michigan	41	0	41
New Hampshire	19	0	19
New York	21	0	21
North Carolina	3,531	3,520	11
Ohio	83	0	83
Pennsylvania	302	0	302
South Carolina	9	6	3
Tennessee	229	0	229
West Virginia	210	0	210
Wisconsin	5	0	5
Total	4,759	3,528	1,231

Table 10—Pulpwood volume by destination, source, and species group, Virginia, 2001[a]

Destination and source	All species	Species group	
		Softwood	Hardwood
	thousand cubic feet		
Virginia (retained)	143,328	72,758	70,570
Exports to:			
Kentucky	4,630	0	4,630
Maryland	7,663	5,444	2,219
North Carolina	9,709	7,962	1,747
Pennsylvania	3,207	2,814	393
South Carolina	344	222	122
Tennessee	1,565	0	1,565
Total	27,118	16,442	10,676
Imports from:			
Delaware	144	35	109
Illinois	2	2	0
Kentucky	77	0	77
Maryland	4,019	1,407	2,612
North Carolina	23,087	5,552	17,535
South Carolina	1	0	1
Tennessee	1	0	1
West Virginia	10,531	289	10,242
Total	37,862	7,285	30,577

[a] Includes roundwood delivered to nonpulpmills, then chipped and sold to pulpmills.

Table 11—Composite panel volume by destination, source, and species group, Virginia, 2001

Destination and source	All species	Species group	
		Softwood	Hardwood
	thousand cubic feet		
Virginia (retained)	33,978	26,107	7,871
Exports to:			
North Carolina	11,102	7,653	3,449
Tennessee	156	152	4
West Virginia	2,609	154	2,455
Total	13,867	7,959	5,908
Imports from:			
North Carolina	3,721	3,563	158
Total	3,721	3,563	158

Table 12—Other industrial volume by destination, source, and species group, Virginia, 2001[a]

Destination and source	All species	Species group	
		Softwood	Hardwood
	thousand cubic feet		
Virginia (retained)	2,202	1,773	429
Exports to:			
Kentucky	86	86	0
North Carolina	19	19	0
Total	105	105	0
Imports from:			
Alabama	152	152	0
Georgia	76	76	0
North Carolina	91	76	15
Total	319	304	15

[a] Includes poles, posts, mulch, firewood, log homes, charcoal, and all other industrial mills.

Table 13—Primary mill residue volume by roundwood type, species group, and residue type, Virginia, 2001

Roundwood type and species group	All types	Residue type			
		Bark	Coarse	Sawdust	Shavings
		thousand cubic feet			
Saw logs					
Softwood	64,210	7,634	28,894	20,170	7,512
Hardwood	81,954	14,431	39,050	28,019	454
Total	146,164	22,065	67,944	48,189	7,966
Veneer logs					
Softwood	9,318	1,252	5,992	2,074	0
Hardwood	516	150	242	124	0
Total	9,834	1,402	6,234	2,198	0
Pulpwood					
Softwood	8,096	8,096	0	0	0
Hardwood	12,576	12,576	0	0	0
Total	20,672	20,672	0	0	0
Composite panels					
Softwood	4,939	4,939	0	0	0
Hardwood	1,803	1,803	0	0	0
Total	6,742	6,742	0	0	0
Other industrial[a]					
Softwood	1,124	957	167	0	0
Hardwood	336	116	172	48	0
Total	1,460	1,073	339	48	0
Total					
Softwood	87,687	22,878	35,053	22,244	7,512
Hardwood	97,185	29,076	39,464	28,191	454
Total	184,872	51,954	74,517	50,435	7,966

[a] Includes poles, pilings, posts, and other industrial products.

Table 14—Disposal of residue at primary wood-using plants by product, species group, and type of residue, Virginia, 1999 and 2001

Product and species group	All types 1999	All types 2001	Bark 1999	Bark 2001	Coarse 1999	Coarse 2001	Sawdust 1999	Sawdust 2001	Shavings 1999	Shavings 2001
					thousand cubic feet					
Fiber products										
Softwood	31,532	33,214	0	0	31,028	32,578	12	12	492	624
Hardwood	28,460	32,046	0	0	27,810	31,537	650	509	0	0
Total	59,992	65,260	0	0	58,838	64,115	662	521	492	624
Particleboard										
Softwood	9,523	6,321	0	0	442	180	5,154	2,389	3,927	3,752
Hardwood	4,376	2,641	0	0	3,284	1,301	1,036	1,311	56	29
Total	13,899	8,962	0	0	3,726	1,481	6,190	3,700	3,983	3,781
Charcoal/ chemical wood										
Softwood	70	109	0	0	0	0	70	109	0	0
Hardwood	722	1,260	27	0	396	419	299	841	0	0
Total	792	1,369	27	0	396	419	369	950	0	0
Sawn products										
Softwood	0	0	0	0	0	0	0	0	0	0
Hardwood	0	0	0	0	0	0	0	0	0	0
Total	0	0	0	0	0	0	0	0	0	0
Fuel										
Softwood	31,375	34,292	13,179	14,394	1,949	1,526	14,726	18,020	1,521	352
Hardwood	31,768	39,543	9,497	15,758	2,506	3,053	19,525	20,430	240	302
Total	63,143	73,835	22,676	30,152	4,455	4,579	34,251	38,450	1,761	654
Miscellaneous										
Softwood	10,892	12,598	6,322	7,821	381	487	2,326	1,506	1,863	2,784
Hardwood	17,806	19,449	11,915	12,535	2,474	2,417	3,293	4,374	124	123
Total	28,698	32,047	18,237	20,356	2,855	2,904	5,619	5,880	1,987	2,907
Not used										
Softwood	1,506	1,154	972	663	308	283	226	208	0	0
Hardwood	3,740	2,246	1,261	783	815	737	1,664	726	0	0
Total	5,246	3,400	2,233	1,446	1,123	1,020	1,890	934	0	0
All products										
Softwood	84,898	87,688	20,473	22,878	34,108	35,054	22,514	22,244	7,803	7,512
Hardwood	86,872	97,185	22,700	29,076	37,285	39,464	26,467	28,191	420	454
Total	171,770	184,873	43,173	51,954	71,393	74,518	48,981	50,435	8,223	7,966

Table 15—Roundwood timber products output by product and species group, Coastal Plain Region of Virginia, 1999 and 2001

Product and species group	Year 1999	Year 2001	Change	Percent change
	thousand cubic feet			
Saw logs				
Softwood	62,254	62,061	-193	-0.3
Hardwood	32,890	33,707	817	2.5
Total	95,144	95,768	624	0.7
Veneer logs				
Softwood	10,378	9,745	-633	-6.1
Hardwood	361	743	382	105.8
Total	10,739	10,488	-251	-2.3
Pulpwood[a]				
Softwood	44,784	53,519	8,735	19.5
Hardwood	24,693	27,394	2,701	10.9
Total	69,477	80,913	11,436	16.5
Composite panels				
Softwood	11,885	11,885	--	--
Hardwood	7,245	7,245	--	--
Total	19,130	19,130	--	--
Other industrial				
Softwood	878	499	-379	-43.2
Hardwood	728	48	-680	-93.4
Total	1,606	547	-1,059	-65.9
All industrial				
Softwood	30,179	137,709	7,530	5.8
Hardwood	65,917	69,137	3,220	4.9
Total	196,096	206,846	10,750	5.5

-- = negligible.

[a] Includes roundwood delivered to nonpulpmills, then chipped and sold to pulpmills (1,599,000 cubic feet in 1999 and 950,000 cubic feet in 2001).

Table 16—Roundwood timber products output by county, product, and species group, Coastal Plain Region of Virginia, 2001

County	All products Soft-wood	All products Hard-wood	Saw logs Soft-wood	Saw logs Hard-wood	Veneer logs Soft-wood	Veneer logs Hard-wood	Pulpwood[a] Soft-wood	Pulpwood[a] Hard-wood	Composite panels Soft-wood	Composite panels Hard-wood	Other industrial Soft-wood	Other industrial Hard-wood
						thousand cubic feet						
Accomack	2,694	679	1,166	184	0	0	1,403	495	0	0	125	0
Brunswick	16,298	6,680	10,115	3,415	1,298	367	4,053	2,391	832	507	0	0
Caroline	7,611	3,591	4,562	2,282	0	0	3,031	1,291	0	0	18	18
Charles City	1,718	1,809	193	967	3	0	1,480	835	0	0	42	7
Chesapeake	754	995	692	287	0	0	62	708	0	0	0	0
Chesterfield	16,126	1,657	1,603	1,230	811	0	13,712	427	0	0	0	0
Dinwiddie	7,272	3,603	3,506	2,236	811	0	2,004	788	951	579	0	0
Essex	4,029	2,037	1,194	916	0	0	2,797	1,114	0	0	38	7
Gloucester	1,763	1,595	646	859	1	0	1,089	736	0	0	27	0
Greensville	8,281	3,706	2,816	1,244	1,298	192	1,196	458	2,971	1,812	0	0
Hampton	7	28	0	0	0	0	7	28	0	0	0	0
Hanover	2,605	1,697	1,329	1,231	0	0	1,271	463	0	0	5	3
Henrico	373	800	27	206	0	0	346	594	0	0	0	0
Isle Of Wight	4,851	4,498	1,462	1,103	811	0	1,152	2,526	1,426	869	0	0
James City	348	547	99	139	0	0	237	408	0	0	12	0
King and Queen	6,010	3,274	1,199	1,548	0	0	4,799	1,726	0	0	12	0
King George	253	1,052	13	957	0	0	235	95	0	0	5	0
King William	2,220	4,186	640	2,644	0	0	1,549	1,542	0	0	31	0
Lancaster	1,195	895	787	479	0	0	359	416	0	0	49	0
Mathews	559	330	391	142	0	0	168	188	0	0	0	0
Middlesex	843	528	470	209	3	0	352	312	0	0	18	7
New Kent	1,410	1,705	327	1,264	0	0	1,067	438	0	0	16	3
Newport News	68	95	10	62	0	0	58	33	0	0	0	0
Northampton	637	339	388	243	0	0	196	96	0	0	53	0
Northumberland	1,283	914	807	599	0	0	469	315	0	0	7	0
Prince George	5,337	1,967	3,330	972	811	0	1,196	992	0	0	0	3
Richmond	1,904	1,183	545	491	0	0	1,343	692	0	0	16	0
Southampton	12,256	6,273	7,067	2,408	1,298	0	2,108	2,778	1,783	1,087	0	0
Suffolk	8,553	3,210	3,715	331	811	0	1,412	1,285	2,615	1,594	0	0
Surry	4,796	3,264	2,492	1,673	811	0	1,493	1,591	0	0	0	0
Sussex	12,933	3,132	8,481	1,238	978	184	2,167	913	1,307	797	0	0
Virginia Beach	287	294	0	13	0	0	287	281	0	0	0	0
Westmoreland	2,354	2,487	1,980	2,099	0	0	349	388	0	0	25	0
York	81	87	9	36	0	0	72	51	0	0	0	0
All counties	137,709	69,137	62,061	33,707	9,745	743	53,519	27,394	11,885	7,245	499	48

[a] Includes roundwood delivered to nonpulpmills, then chipped and sold to pulpmills (950,000 cubic feet in 2001).

Table 17—Roundwood timber products output by product and species group, Southern Piedmont Region of Virginia, 1999 and 2001

Product and species group	Year			Percent change
	1999	2001	Change	
	thousand cubic feet			
Saw logs				
Softwood	31,962	32,737	775	2.4
Hardwood	37,673	38,399	726	1.9
Total	69,635	71,136	1,501	2.2
Veneer logs				
Softwood	3,485	3,246	-239	-6.9
Hardwood	900	683	-217	-24.1
Total	4,385	3,929	-456	-10.4
Pulpwood[a]				
Softwood	38,303	23,141	-15,162	-39.6
Hardwood	29,847	27,514	-2,333	-7.8
Total	68,150	50,655	-17,495	-25.7
Composite panels				
Softwood	16,764	19,963	3,199	19.1
Hardwood	2,224	3,528	1,304	58.6
Total	18,988	23,491	4,503	23.7
Other industrial				
Softwood	394	270	-124	-31.5
Hardwood	1,502	76	-1,426	-94.9
Total	1,896	346	-1,550	-81.8
All industrial				
Softwood	90,908	79,357	-11,551	-12.7
Hardwood	72,146	70,200	-1,946	-2.7
Total	163,054	149,557	-13,497	-8.3

[a] Includes roundwood delivered to nonpulpmills, then chipped and sold to pulpmills (1,768,000 cubic feet in 1999 and 1,547,000 cubic feet in 2001).

Table 18—Roundwood timber products output by county, product, and species group, Southern Piedmont Region of Virginia, 2001

County	All products		Saw logs		Veneer logs		Pulpwood[a]		Composite panels		Other industrial	
	Soft-wood	Hard-wood	Soft-wood	Hard-wood	Soft-wood	Hard-wood	Soft-wood	Hard-wood	Soft-wood	Hard-wood	Soft-wood	Hard-wood
	thousand cubic feet											
Amelia	5,134	3,557	2,172	1,990	811	0	2,151	1,567	0	0	0	0
Appomattox	4,040	2,733	666	1,352	0	5	1,898	1,376	1,476	0	0	0
Bedford	2,833	4,711	763	3,197	0	3	594	1,511	1,476	0	0	0
Buckingham	4,902	4,617	1,826	1,330	0	0	3,076	3,287	0	0	0	0
Campbell	4,801	3,638	1,794	2,119	0	2	1,531	1,517	1,476	0	0	0
Charlotte	5,411	7,705	1,961	5,022	0	0	1,823	2,637	1,627	39	0	7
Cumberland	1,291	1,409	173	659	1	0	853	739	0	0	264	11
Franklin	3,937	5,751	1,188	3,943	0	3	1,273	1,805	1,476	0	0	0
Halifax	10,510	5,940	5,376	2,278	0	430	1,211	2,506	3,923	704	0	22
Henry	3,926	4,772	1,951	1,959	0	99	1,200	1,980	775	727	0	7
Lunenburg	6,644	3,954	2,324	1,724	811	0	1,213	1,596	2,296	634	0	0
Mecklenburg	5,622	3,938	1,987	2,537	811	50	1,283	1,097	1,541	254	0	0
Nottoway	5,249	1,742	3,245	1,331	811	91	1,193	320	0	0	0	0
Patrick	1,780	5,091	848	3,946	0	0	151	472	775	673	6	0
Pittsylvania	10,052	6,094	4,367	2,197	0	0	2,563	3,378	3,122	497	0	22
Powhatan	1,566	1,378	1,238	942	1	0	327	429	0	0	0	7
Prince Edward	1,659	3,170	858	1,873	0	0	801	1,297	0	0	0	0
All counties	79,357	70,200	32,737	38,399	3,246	683	23,141	27,514	19,963	3,528	270	76

[a] Includes roundwood delivered to nonpulpmills, then chipped and sold to pulpmills (1,547,000 cubic feet in 2001).

Table 19—Roundwood timber products output by product and species group, Northern Piedmont Region of Virginia, 1999 and 2001

Product and species group	Year		Change	Percent change
	1999	2001		
	thousand cubic feet			
Saw logs				
Softwood	9,616	7,395	-2,221	-23.1
Hardwood	16,116	15,756	-360	-2.2
Total	25,732	23,151	-2,581	-10.0
Veneer logs				
Softwood	0	0	0	--
Hardwood	802	555	-247	-30.8
Total	802	555	-247	-30.8
Pulpwood[a]				
Softwood	11,780	9,715	-2,065	-17.5
Hardwood	9,146	9,153	7	0.1
Total	20,926	18,868	-2,058	-9.8
Composite panels				
Softwood	1,722	1,476	-246	-14.3
Hardwood	69	0	-69	-100.0
Total	1,791	1,476	-315	-17.6
Other industrial				
Softwood	937	930	-7	-0.7
Hardwood	234	248	14	6.0
Total	1,171	1,178	7	0.6
All industrial				
Softwood	24,055	19,516	-4,539	-18.9
Hardwood	26,367	25,712	-655	-2.5
Total	50,422	45,228	-5,194	-10.3

-- = negligible.

[a] Includes roundwood delivered to nonpulpmills, then chipped and sold to pulpmills (246,000 cubic feet in 1999 and 137,000 cubic feet in 2001).

Table 20—Roundwood timber products output by county, product, and species group, Northern Piedmont Region of Virginia, 2001

County	All products		Saw logs		Veneer logs		Pulpwood[a]		Composite panels		Other industrial	
	Soft-wood	Hard-wood	Soft-wood	Hard-wood	Soft-wood	Hard-wood	Soft-wood	Hard-wood	Soft-wood	Hard-wood	Soft-wood	Hard-wood
	thousand cubic feet											
Albemarle	2,226	2,183	1,645	1,666	0	0	537	517	0	0	44	0
Amherst	2,796	3,329	294	2,602	0	0	974	727	1,476	0	52	0
Culpeper	803	1,790	172	1,093	0	0	582	602	0	0	49	95
Fairfax	219	450	2	386	0	5	217	59	0	0	0	0
Fauquier	568	918	171	460	0	0	397	458	0	0	0	0
Fluvanna	1,322	423	708	98	0	0	599	325	0	0	15	0
Goochland	1,130	962	534	180	0	0	596	782	0	0	0	0
Greene	128	426	14	357	0	0	1	32	0	0	113	37
Loudoun	15	2,104	3	696	0	530	12	878	0	0	0	0
Louisa	3,638	3,406	1,290	1,954	0	0	1,890	1,406	0	0	458	46
Madison	170	1,074	41	1,028	0	0	23	46	0	0	106	0
Nelson	1,662	3,469	268	2,549	0	0	1,394	920	0	0	0	0
Orange	1,344	1,206	880	777	0	7	371	384	0	0	93	38
Prince William	159	295	0	88	0	0	159	207	0	0	0	0
Rappahannock	68	682	0	445	0	13	68	224	0	0	0	0
Spotsylvania	2,628	1,774	1,099	611	0	0	1,529	1,131	0	0	0	32
Stafford	640	1,221	274	766	0	0	366	455	0	0	0	0
All counties	19,516	25,712	7,395	15,756	0	555	9,715	9,153	1,476	0	930	248

[a] Includes roundwood delivered to nonpulpmills, then chipped and sold to pulpmills (137,000 cubic feet in 2001).

Table 21—Roundwood timber products output by product and species group, Northern Mountain Region of Virginia, 1999 and 2001

Product and species group	Year			
	1999	2001	Change	Percent change
	thousand cubic feet			
Saw logs				
Softwood	1,261	1,250	-11	-0.9
Hardwood	15,142	15,078	-64	-0.4
Total	16,403	16,328	-75	-0.5
Veneer logs				
Softwood	--	--	--	--
Hardwood	327	53	-274	-83.8
Total	327	53	-274	-83.8
Pulpwood[a]				
Softwood	2,595	2,632	37	1.4
Hardwood	8,284	9,212	928	11.2
Total	10,879	11,844	965	8.9
Composite panels				
Softwood	0	44	44	--
Hardwood	0	1,431	1,431	--
Total	0	1,475	1,475	--
Other industrial				
Softwood	114	79	-35	-30.7
Hardwood	57	57	--	--
Total	171	136	-35	-20.5
All industrial				
Softwood	3,970	4,005	35	0.9
Hardwood	23,810	25,831	2,021	8.5
Total	27,780	29,836	2,056	7.4

-- = negligible.

[a] Includes roundwood delivered to nonpulpmills, then chipped and sold to pulpmills (13,000 cubic feet in 1999 and 16,000 cubic feet in 2001).

Table 22—Roundwood timber products output by county, product, and species group, Northern Mountain Region of Virginia, 2001

County	All products		Saw logs		Veneer logs		Pulpwood[a]		Composite panels		Other industrial	
	Soft-wood	Hard-wood	Soft-wood	Hard-wood	Soft-wood	Hard-wood	Soft-wood	Hard-wood	Soft-wood	Hard-wood	Soft-wood	Hard-wood
						thousand cubic feet							
Alleghany	920	4,697	419	2,059	0	3	457	2,026	44	609	0	0
Augusta	738	3,010	365	1,875	0	0	373	1,116	0	0	0	19
Bath	325	2,196	68	813	0	0	257	1,383	0	0	0	0
Botetourt	493	2,688	22	1,076	0	2	471	1,610	0	0	0	0
Clarke	7	749	2	738	0	8	5	3	0	0	0	0
Craig	124	444	4	41	0	0	120	403	0	0	0	0
Frederick	318	1,909	35	1,662	0	10	283	237	0	0	0	0
Highland	124	2,603	0	964	0	0	124	817	0	822	0	0
Page	0	156	0	156	0	0	0	0	0	0	0	0
Roanoke	233	520	147	345	0	0	86	175	0	0	0	0
Rockbridge	447	3,840	129	2,870	0	16	239	935	0	0	79	19
Rockingham	126	1,244	52	983	0	0	74	242	0	0	0	19
Shenandoah	127	921	6	772	0	6	121	143	0	0	0	0
Warren	23	854	1	724	0	8	22	122	0	0	0	0
All counties	4,005	25,831	1,250	15,078	0	53	2,632	9,212	44	1,431	79	57

[a] Includes roundwood delivered to nonpulpmills, then chipped and sold to pulpmills (16,000 cubic feet in 2001)

Table 23—Roundwood timber products output by product and species group, Southern Mountain Region of Virginia, 1999 and 2001

Product and species group	Year 1999	2001	Change	Percent change
	thousand cubic feet			
Saw logs				
Softwood	10,206	12,260	2,054	20.1
Hardwood	28,757	33,789	5,032	17.5
Total	38,963	46,049	7,086	18.2
Veneer logs				
Softwood	84	84	--	--
Hardwood	3,557	3,776	219	6.2
Total	3,641	3,860	219	6.0
Pulpwood[a]				
Softwood	202	193	-9	-4.5
Hardwood	5,566	7,973	2,407	43.2
Total	5,768	8,166	2,398	41.6
Composite panels				
Softwood	735	698	-37	-5.0
Hardwood	5,014	1,575	-3,439	-68.6
Total	5,749	2,273	-3,476	-60.5
Other industrial				
Softwood	88	100	12	13.6
Hardwood	--	--	--	--
Total	88	100	12	13.6
All industrial				
Softwood	11,315	13,335	2,020	17.9
Hardwood	42,894	47,113	4,219	9.8
Total	54,209	60,448	6,239	11.5

-- = negligible.

[a] Includes roundwood delivered to nonpulpmills, then chipped and sold to pulpmills (67,000 cubic feet in 1999 and 84,000 cubic feet in 2001).

Table 24—Roundwood timber products output by county, product, and species group, Southern Mountain Region of Virginia, 2001

County	All products		Saw logs		Veneer logs		Pulpwood[a]		Composite panels		Other industrial	
	Soft-wood	Hard-wood	Soft-wood	Hard-wood	Soft-wood	Hard-wood	Soft-wood	Hard-wood	Soft-wood	Hard-wood	Soft-wood	Hard-wood
	thousand cubic feet											
Bland	367	2,135	313	1,586	0	0	0	23	54	526	0	0
Buchanan	1,417	1,052	1,413	978	0	70	4	4	0	0	0	0
Carroll	5,559	5,471	5,261	5,078	0	46	62	151	230	196	6	0
Dickenson	88	8,547	0	2,337	0	46	0	6,164	0	0	88	0
Floyd	1,734	2,174	1,612	1,881	0	12	18	183	104	98	0	0
Giles	255	2,700	201	2,025	0	45	0	118	54	512	0	0
Grayson	1,217	3,335	1,210	3,076	0	0	1	259	0	0	6	0
Lee	418	3,684	334	2,178	84	1,490	0	16	0	0	0	0
Montgomery	110	1,013	93	775	0	0	17	238	0	0	0	0
Pulaski	196	536	23	495	0	0	69	18	104	23	0	0
Russell	0	2,308	0	1,698	0	609	0	1	0	0	0	0
Scott	815	4,138	663	3,759	0	374	0	1	152	4	0	0
Smyth	4	1,276	4	772	0	70	0	218	0	216	0	0
Tazewell	22	700	0	408	0	0	22	292	0	0	0	0
Washington	16	1,229	16	1,056	0	46	0	127	0	0	0	0
Wise	219	2,557	219	1,705	0	851	0	1	0	0	0	0
Wythe	898	4,258	898	3,982	0	117	0	159	0	0	0	0
All counties	13,335	47,113	12,260	33,789	84	3,776	193	7,973	698	1,575	100	0

[a] Includes roundwood delivered to nonpulpmills, then chipped and sold to pulpmills (84,000 cubic feet in 2001)

Table 25—Total roundwood output by product, species group, and source of material, Virginia, 2001

Product and species group	All sources	Total	Growing-stock trees		Other sources
			Sawtimber	Poletimber	
	thousand cubic feet				
Saw logs					
Softwood	115,703	112,956	108,452	4,504	2,747
Hardwood	136,729	128,210	121,454	6,757	8,519
Total	252,432	241,167	229,906	11,261	11,265
Veneer logs and bolts					
Softwood	13,075	12,921	12,662	259	154
Hardwood	5,810	5,760	5,523	237	50
Total	18,885	18,681	18,185	495	204
Pulpwood					
Softwood	89,200	80,067	36,830	43,236	9,133
Hardwood	81,246	72,183	32,482	39,701	9,063
Total	170,446	152,250	69,313	82,937	18,196
Composite panels					
Softwood	34,066	30,578	14,066	16,512	3,488
Hardwood	13,779	12,242	5,509	6,733	1,537
Total	47,845	42,820	19,575	23,245	5,025
Poles and posts					
Softwood	1,781	1,462	1,336	126	319
Hardwood	69	58	42	16	11
Total	1,850	1,521	1,379	142	329
Other miscellaneous					
Softwood	97	97	69	28	0
Hardwood	360	328	234	94	32
Total	457	425	303	122	32
Total industrial products					
Softwood	253,922	238,081	173,416	64,666	15,841
Hardwood	237,993	218,782	165,245	53,538	19,211
Total	491,915	456,863	338,660	118,203	35,052
Fuelwood					
Softwood	5,147	4,684	3,374	1,310	463
Hardwood	46,148	41,489	29,892	11,597	4,660
Total	51,295	46,172	33,266	12,906	5,123
All products					
Softwood	259,069	242,765	176,789	65,975	16,304
Hardwood	284,141	260,271	195,136	65,134	23,870
Total	543,210	503,035	371,926	131,110	40,175

Numbers in rows and columns may not sum to totals due to rounding.

Table 26—Total roundwood output by species group, survey region, and ownership class, Virginia, 2001

Species group and survey region	Total	Ownership class		
		Public	Forest industry	Nonindustrial private
		thousand cubic feet		
Softwoods				
Coastal Plain	140,500	3,927	24,662	111,911
Southern Piedmont	80,966	733	12,311	67,922
Northern Piedmont	19,911	423	3,554	15,934
Northern Mountains	4,088	1,915	0	2,173
Southern Mountains	13,604	0	184	13,420
Total softwoods	259,069	6,997	40,711	211,361
Hardwoods				
Coastal Plain	82,541	599	8,593	73,349
Southern Piedmont	83,812	1,599	9,884	72,330
Northern Piedmont	30,698	0	3,087	27,611
Northern Mountains	30,841	10,048	1,583	19,210
Southern Mountains	56,249	963	3,643	51,643
Total hardwoods	284,141	13,208	26,790	244,142
All species	543,210	20,206	67,502	455,503

Numbers in rows and columns may not sum to totals due to rounding.

Table 27—Total roundwood output by species group, detailed species group, and product, Virginia, 2001

Species group and detailed species group	Total	Product						
		Saw log	Veneer	Pulpwood	Composite panel	Poles and posts	Other miscellaneous	Fuel-wood
				thousand cubic feet				
Softwood								
Cedar	991	230	29	496	123	6	88	19
White pine	9,942	7,101	0	947	1,680	16	0	198
Loblolly-shortleaf pine	181,821	79,562	12,524	63,529	21,579	1,006	9	3,612
Other yellow pines	62,969	25,670	509	24,186	10,603	750	0	1,251
Cypress	127	72	13	21	18	0	0	3
Hemlock	3,219	3,067	0	21	63	3	0	64
Total softwoods	259,069	115,703	13,075	89,200	34,066	1,781	97	5,147
Hardwood								
Soft maple	20,519	9,554	866	5,362	1,392	4	10	3,332
Hard maple	2,232	818	95	844	113	0	0	363
Other birch	2,844	1,392	15	856	119	1	0	462
Hickory	14,912	7,536	451	4,206	280	4	13	2,422
Beech	4,292	1,638	112	1,625	220	0	0	697
Ash	3,638	1,573	210	1,059	203	0	1	591
Black walnut	2,415	1,346	56	599	21	0	2	392
Sweetgum	21,456	8,423	268	7,497	1,758	10	16	3,484
Yellow-poplar	54,769	26,062	1,086	16,105	2,557	18	46	8,895
Blackgum-tupelo	5,093	2,147	94	1,596	401	1	27	827
Sycamore	3,086	1,231	116	974	261	1	1	501
Cottonwood	509	227	2	164	32	0	0	83
Black cherry	750	371	1	252	2	0	1	122
Select white oaks	45,090	20,655	409	14,183	2,399	12	109	7,323
Other white oaks	20,243	10,215	284	5,852	578	0	26	3,288
Select red oaks	19,336	9,587	263	5,081	1,251	2	13	3,141
Other red oaks	49,210	26,215	1,047	12,151	1,738	15	51	7,993
Basswood	1,578	727	56	535	0	0	4	256
Elm	1,172	511	10	395	65	0	0	190
Other Eastern hardwoods	10,996	6,500	369	1,910	390	1	39	1,786
Total hardwoods	284,141	136,729	5,810	81,246	13,779	69	360	46,148
All species	543,210	252,432	18,885	170,446	47,845	1,850	457	51,295

Numbers in rows and columns may not sum to totals due to rounding

Table 28—Total roundwood output by species group, detailed species group, and ownership class, Virginia, 2001

Species group and detailed species group	Total	Ownership class		
		Public	Forest industry	Nonindustrial private
	thousand cubic feet			
Softwood				
Cedar	991	89	62	840
White pine	9,942	10	200	9,732
Loblolly-shortleaf pine	181,821	2,872	30,584	148,366
Other yellow pines	62,969	4,026	9,794	49,149
Cypress	127	0	40	86
Hemlock	3,219	0	31	3,188
Total softwoods	259,069	6,997	40,711	211,361
Hardwood				
Soft maple	20,519	2,047	1,677	16,795
Hard maple	2,232	0	50	2,182
Other birch	2,844	40	34	2,770
Hickory	14,912	262	1,575	13,075
Beech	4,292	0	199	4,093
Ash	3,638	30	461	3,147
Black walnut	2,415	86	25	2,304
Sweetgum	21,456	183	2,312	18,960
Yellow-poplar	54,769	884	5,442	48,444
Blackgum-tupelo	5,093	148	491	4,454
Sycamore	3,086	0	114	2,971
Cottonwood	509	0	37	472
Black cherry	750	16	101	633
Select white oaks	45,090	1,102	5,575	38,413
Other white oaks	20,243	2,861	2,521	14,861
Select red oaks	19,336	2,286	1,374	15,676
Other red oaks	49,210	2,874	4,062	42,274
Basswood	1,578	193	52	1,333
Elm	1,172	5	188	979
Other Eastern hardwoods	10,996	190	500	10,306
Total hardwoods	284,141	13,208	26,790	244,142
All species	543,210	20,206	67,502	455,503

Numbers in rows and columns may not sum to totals due to rounding.

www.ingramcontent.com/pod-product-compliance
Lightning Source LLC
Chambersburg PA
CBHW080624290526
45790CB00007B/2910